DATE DUE			
JE 15 '94			
JE 17 '94			

D1307661

A WETLAND WALK

written and illustrated by SHERI AMSEL

THE MILLBROOK PRESS

Brookfield, Connecticut

A LUCAS • EVANS BOOK

Library of Congress Cataloging-in-Publication Data
Amsel, Sheri. A wetland walk / by Sheri Amsel.
p. cm. *Summary: Illustrations and rhyming text depict a day-long walk*
through a marsh and introduce the plants and animals of a wetland
environment.
ISBN 1-56294-213-1 1. Wetlands—Juvenile literature. 2. Wetland fauna—Juvenile
literature. 3. Wetland flora—Juvenile literature. [1. Marsh
animals. 2. Marsh plants. 3. Wetland ecology. 4. Ecology.] I. Title.
QH87.3.A47 1993 574.909′69—dc20 92-5105 CIP AC

5 3 1 2 4

*For my husband, Richard, who showed me
the great adventure of exploring wetlands.*

Once I spent a day outside,
to wander through a marshy tide.

Flowers grow on the water's edge,
A pickerel weed, a grassy sedge.

A dragonfly, on sparkling wings,
whizzes by—his body sings.

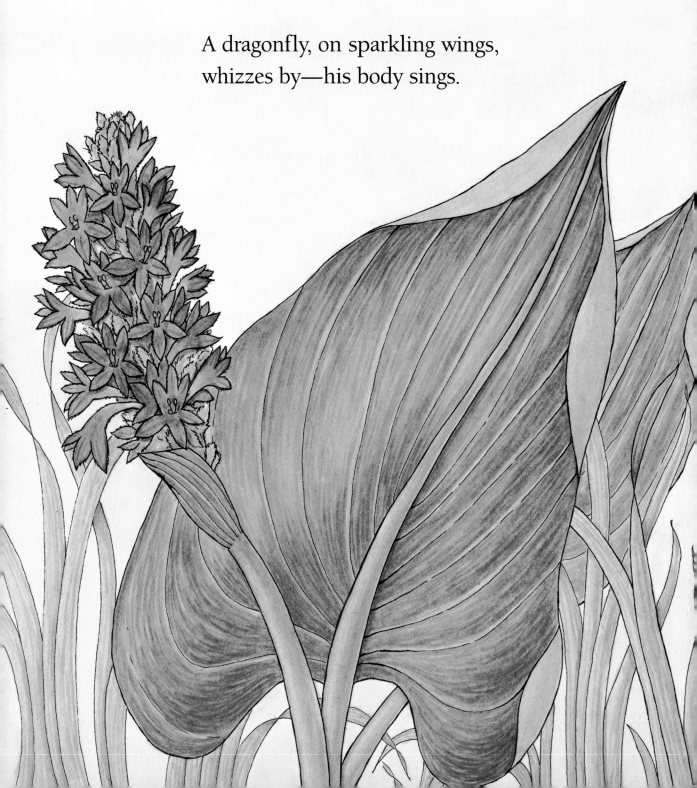

A frog dives, leaving silver rings;
a tadpole swims, a peeper sings.

An osprey swoops, its prey in sight,
a fish in claws, its meal that night.

I rest on moss so soft and green,
and watch a pintail stop to preen.

Mosquitoes buzz around my head.
I wave my arms and watch them spread.

The swamp is filled with buzzing sound;
on hands and knees I look around.

A Venus's-flytrap opens wide—
a bee flies in, gets trapped inside.

Spiders spin from leaf and vine,
cling to webs on spruce and pine.

Fly in a web, as strong as steel;
the spider jumps, a tasty meal.

A raccoon chews fish in his jaws;
he sniffs the air and licks his paws.

A loon calls softly from across the bog
and dives for fish underneath a log.

A mayfly dances for a mate,
the sky glows red, it's getting late.

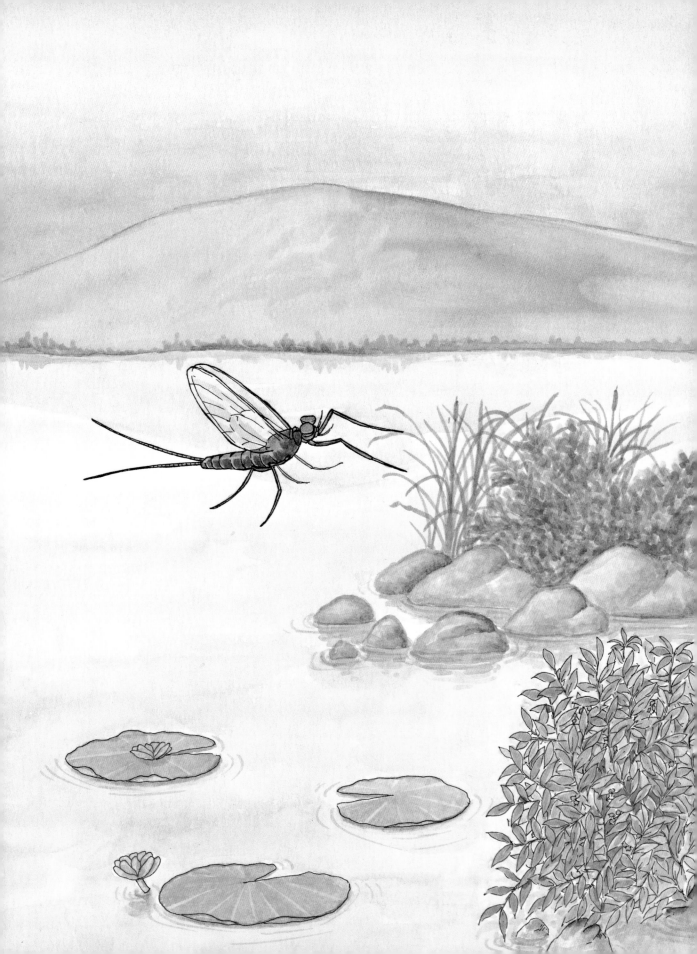

The reeds and cattails bend and sway,
to greet with joy the end of day.

I make my way back around the bog,
nestled in its nightly fog.

FACTS ABOUT WETLANDS

Are marshes, swamps, and bogs the same?
No. *Marshes* usually form near ponds and lakes. Reeds, grasses, and other soft-stemmed plants grow there. Trees and woody-stemmed shrubs grow in *swamps*. Sometimes the growth is so thick that it's hard to walk through a swamp.

Bogs begin as shallow ponds that slowly fill with rotting leaves. Then mosses and other plants spread out from the shore across the surface of the bog, forming a thick mat.

Is it true that something that falls into a bog won't rot?
The remains of animals hundreds and even thousands of years old have been found in the mucky depths of bogs. This is because rotting, or decay, takes place very slowly in a bog. Plant growth seals the bog's surface. Underneath, lack of air and acids from plants slow the process of decay.

Why do some wetland plants eat insects?
Most plants get all the energy they need from sunlight and nutrients in the soil. But in wetlands, water often washes nutrients out of the soil. Insects provide some plants with those missing nutrients.

Why are wetlands so noisy in spring?
Frogs and birds call to attract mates and to mark off their territories. In North America, tiny frogs called spring peepers are usually the first to call—a sure sign of spring.

Why are wetlands important to wildlife?
Wetlands provide homes for many kinds of plants and animals. Frogs, dragonflies, mosquitoes, and many other creatures lay their eggs and spend the first stages of their lives in the water. They provide food for fish. And the fish provide food for many of the birds and mammals that live in wetlands.

Why are wetlands important to people?
Besides providing homes for wildlife, wetlands absorb flood waters and help prevent land from washing away. They filter sewage and other pollutants from water. And water from wetlands helps maintain the water table—the underground water supply that many cities rely on. Finally, wetlands are beautiful—and that makes them valuable, too.

A wetland is a wonderful place to search and discover. Anywhere there is deep water or tangles of brush, however, a child should bring along an adult.